1 MONTH OF
FREE
READING

at
www.ForgottenBooks.com

By purchasing this book you are eligible for one month membership to ForgottenBooks.com, giving you unlimited access to our entire collection of over 1,000,000 titles via our web site and mobile apps.

To claim your free month visit:
www.forgottenbooks.com/free642616

ISBN 978-0-484-61721-5
PIBN 10642616

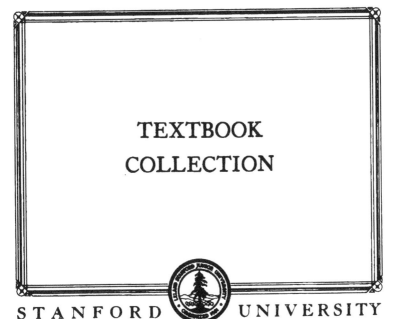

carpenter   barber

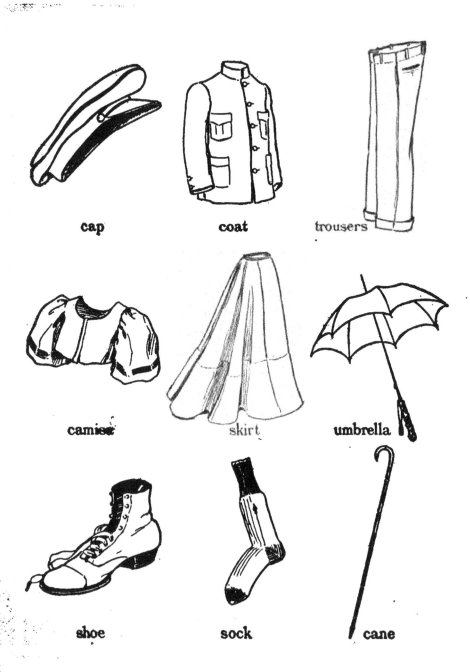

cap   coat   trousers

camise   skirt   umbrella

shoe   sock   cane

This is an easy first book incorporating The Philippine Chart, with additional lessons in reading, writing, drawing, conversation, and many devices to employ the pupils at their seats.

The PHILIPPINE CHART PRIMER

BY
MARY E. COLEMAN
MARGARET PURCELL
O. S. REIMOLD
JOHN W. RITCHIE

NEW YORK & MANILA
WORLD BOOK COMPANY
1906

PHILIPPINE EDUCATION SERIES

The Philippine Chart. By Mary E. Coleman, Margaret A. Purcell, and O. S. Reimold.

The Philippine Chart Primer. By Mary E. Coleman, Margaret A. Purcell, O. S. Reimold, and John W. Ritchie.

First Year Book. By Mary H. Fee, Margaret A. Purcell, Parker H. Fillmore, and John W. Ritchie.

Primary Arithmetic: Parts I and II. By Mabel Bonsall.

Primary Arithmetic: Part III. *Revised Edition.* By Mabel Bonsall and George E. Mercer.

Complete Arithmetic: Part I. By George E. Mercer and Mabel Bonsall.

First Primary Language Book. By O. S. Reimold.

Second Primary Language Book. By O. S. Reimold.

Composition Leaflets on Philippine Activities. By O. S. Reimold.

Stories of Long Ago in the Philippines. By D. O. McGovney.

Animal Studies. By Edgar M. Ledyard.

Physiology and Hygiene. By John W. Ritchie.

The Filipino Teacher's Manual. By H. C. Theobald.

Graphic Outline Maps. By Caspar W. Hodgson.

World Book Co., Park Hill, Yonkers, New York.

129458
C

TO THE TEACHER

THIS book is intended for the resourceless, restless little pupil who is compelled to sit idle after his lesson is done. You have often wondered how to keep him quiet, and he has often wondered if the hour for dismissal would ever come. To enable you to do your work in peace and to enable him to advance happily and rapidly along the road to knowledge, this little book has been written.

The Philippine Chart Primer contains the 32 lessons of The Philippine Chart and six additional lessons, giving a total of 87 word forms which the pupils will learn from the printed page. There is a script alphabet on page 39 which will furnish models for the letter forms of all writing exercises. The drawings on pages 42 to 48 develop the four simplest type forms, and furnish the basis of a course in drawing. Page 48 gives a simple kind of action drawing easy for pupils to do. Other drawing exercises, also reduced to the utmost simplicity, will be found distributed throughout the book. Drawings thus placed directly before the pupils are greatly superior to blackboard models, which only the few directly in front of the board can see at a correct angle.

The first two pages of the book, pages 49 to 53, and the last two pages provide nine picture pages for conversational work. Here are 81 pictures illustrating objects, actions, and occupations known to every child, each with the name clearly printed under it. Pupils may copy the words in script and draw the simple, clear-cut pictures; in this way it is believed that they will learn without any effort on the part of the teacher most of the 87 printed words on these pages. Many additional words may be learned orally through the unlimited conversational work these pages suggest.

The seat work suggestions found at the end of each reading lesson will not only keep pupils busy, but teach them manual dexterity and neatness, accuracy of measurement, and keenness of observation. The materials needed for this work are everywhere abundant in the Philippines. Bamboo sticks or matches will be needed for the stick laying ; bejuco, buri, paper, long grass, strips of palm leaves, and bamboo can all be used for the various weaving and braiding exercises. Use seeds and sections of bamboo or camoting-cahoy and perforated shells for stringing necklaces ; make tablets from match boxes and the backs of writing pads. Many exercises are interchangeable ; for instance, the stick laying exercises may also be drawn, or the bird's nest may first be modeled in clay, and then woven of grass or bejuco. The work will be made interesting to children if the materials be colored. This may be done by using native dye woods and colored crayons. Utilize the help of the older pupils in procuring and preparing materials, and also in distributing and collecting them for each class exercise. Teach the children to take care of the materials and to keep them clean. Whenever it is possible, let them take home their work ; this will stimulate their interest and encourage them to do their best.

This book is designed to accompany and fix the work of the chart and to prepare the pupil by the end of the first half year for his regular First Year Book.

a

a

a

Stick laying.   Read pages vii, viii.

a

a

a

a

Paper folding and tearing.   Read pages vii, viii.

This is a

This is a

This is a

This is a

This is a

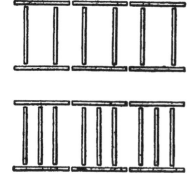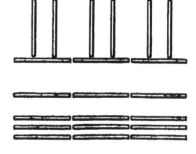

I have a

I have a

I have a

I have a

This is a

I have a

Drawing. See pages 40, 41.

I have a

This is my

This is my

This is a

This is my

I have my

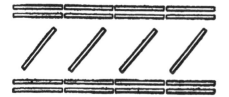 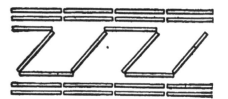

. Color the sticks to make the designs more attractive.

You have a

You have my

This is a

This is my

I have a

You have a

Folding a fan.   Making a round fan.

I can see a

You can see a

This is a

You can see my

I can see my

You have a

I have a

Drawing.   See pages 40, 41.

You have a

This is your

I can see your

You can see my

I have a

You can see a

I have your

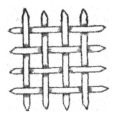  

Splint weaving.   Use bamboo strips, bejuco, or grasses.

I can see the

You can see the

You can see the

I have a

This is my

You have the

I see your

Modeling of clay or dough. Read pages vii, viii.

This is a

You can see this

I can see this

You have this

I see the

You have my

This is your

Making a book. Fold the paper, cut the leaves, and tie with string or grass.

I can see this

I can see this boy.

You have a

You have a dog.

This is your

This is your cat.

You can see the

You can see the girl.

boy   dog   cat

From now on have pupils do some writing each lesson.
See page 39.

The boy can run.

The girl can run.

Your dog can run.

This cat can run.

My cat can run.

I can run.

You can run.

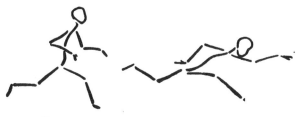

See page 48.

I have a [image: vase] and a [image: plate]

You see a [image: book] and a [image: hat]

I see my [image: leaf] and my [image: ball]

I have a cat and a [image: goat]

I have a cat and a goat.

My cat and my goat can run.

A boy and a dog can run.

Knot tying. Use string or grasses. Tie knots at equal intervals. See pages vii, viii.

You have one

I have two

I can see two

You can see one

You have two

This is one goat.

Your goat can run.

String pieces of bamboo or reed. Pieces should be of equal length. They may be colored.

The boy can jump.

The dog can jump.

My goat can jump.

Your cat can jump.

This boy can run and jump.

A goat and a dog can jump.

You can run and I can jump.

The boy has one

The girl has two

I have one

You have two

The girl has a

The boy has this

I have a   and a

Encourage pupils to make similar designs of their own.

16

The boy has a

He has a

He has this and

He can see two

He can run and jump.

This is my

I can see one

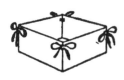 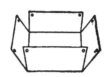 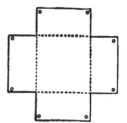

Make a paper box.

The girl has a

She has a and a

She has two

She can see one

The boy can see this

He can see your ball.

You have my ball and my

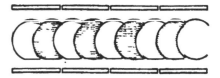

Tablet laying.   Tablets may be made of buri, match boxes, backs of writing pads.

The boy can throw the ball.

He can throw the ball.

The boy can catch the ball.

He can run and catch a ball.

You can throw your ball.

I can catch my ball.

The boy can throw a

Juan is a boy.

He has a

This is his

Juan can see his

He can catch his

I see my and his dog.

Juan has this basket.

After the paper has been torn, faces may be drawn.

20

Maria has one

This is her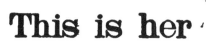

She can see her

I see her jar and her cat.

Her cat can run.

She has her jar and her

Juan has a goat.

His goat can jump.

Keep both strings together and tie the knots at equal distances.

Maria has a cat.

Her cat is in my hat.

My cat is in your basket.

Juan has a dog.

His dog is in the box.

I see his dog in the box.

One jar is in the box.

The girl can carry a jar.

Juan can carry a basket.

He has a  in his basket.

Maria can carry a slate.

She has a slate and a

I can throw this

You can catch my mango.

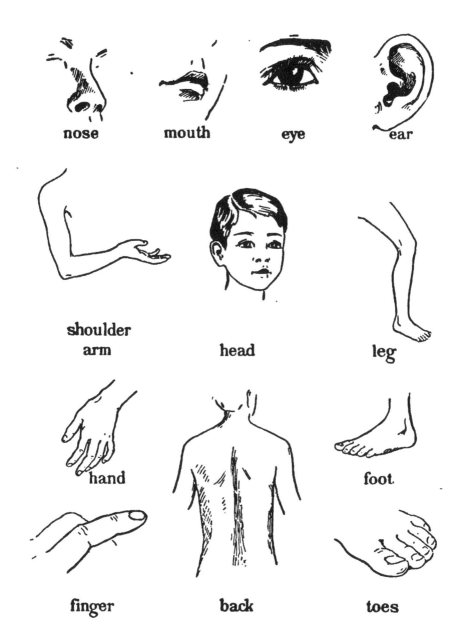

nose   mouth   eye   ear

shoulder
arm   head   leg

hand   foot.

finger   back   toes

Use this page for conversation work. The children may draw some of the simpler pictures and copy the words under them.

24

Maria has two hands.

She has a book in one hand.

I see a book in her hand.

Maria has two feet.

She can run and jump.

I have two hands and two feet.

I can carry my slate.

Juan can catch a mango.

Making paper chain. The links should be of uniform width and length.

I see a boy and his kite.

The kite can fly.

You can see this

The bird can fly.

A bird and a kite can fly.

Juan can see his kite fly.

He can see the bird fly.

Modeling and drawing.

26

The big boy can throw a ball.

The big goat can jump.

The little goat can run.

The little girl has a book.

She has a book and a fan.

You can see her little fan.

I can carry a big box.

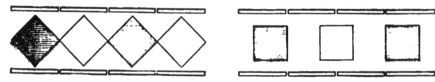

Tablet laying. Read page 18. Tablets may be colored.

This is a big table.

My hat is on the table.

Your mango is on the table.

A basket is under the table.

A big  is in the basket.

A  is under the table.

A jar is under the table.

I see Juan and his dog.

Juan can swim.

I see his hands and feet.

The dog can swim.

You can see a big fish.

The big fish can swim.

Can the little fly?

I see two baskets.

One basket is round.

One basket is square.

My little basket is square.

Your big basket is round.

Maria has a round box.

Her round box is little.

Juan has a square box.

What is in the square box?

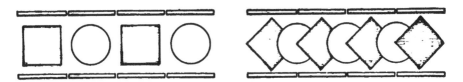

Lay the sticks and tablets on slates and outline the design.

What has Juan in his hand?

He gives Maria the book.

Maria takes the book.

Juan gives Maria his book.

Maria takes his book.

Juan gives Maria a

Maria takes the banana.

Three-strand plaiting.   Use string or grasses.

Juan has a big banana.
He can eat the banana.
He gives Maria the mango.
Maria takes the mango.
She can eat the mango.
The cat is under the table.
The cat can eat the fish.
What can the bird eat?

Let the pupils tear in simple outline other animals.

What is in the jar?

Water is in the jar.

Juan gives the bird water.

The bird drinks water.

The dog drinks water.

You and I drink water.

The dog swims in water.

The fish swims in water.

See pages 44, 46.

What has the little boy?
He has a banana and a
I can see his knife.
He cuts the banana.
What has the big boy?
He has a knife and a stick.
He cuts the stick.
Can you cut a big stick?

Both the single and double knots should be at equal distances.

Maria has rice in her hand.

She gives the bird rice.

The bird eats the rice.

The boy cuts the grass.

Juan gives the carabao grass.

The carabao eats grass.

The carabao drinks water.

Juan and Maria eat rice.

Four-strand plaiting.

Is the fish in the water?

Yes, the fish is in the water.

Is the boy in the water?

No, he is not in the water.

Can the boy catch the fish?

No, he cannot catch the fish.

Can the fish swim?

Yes, the fish can swim.

For additional drawing work, see pages 40–48.

Juan is playing.
He plays with the kite.
He is flying his kite.

Is this boy playing?
Yes, he plays with the stick.

Is Maria playing with a kite?
No, she is playing with a ball.
Is the little cat playing?
Yes, she is playing with a ball.

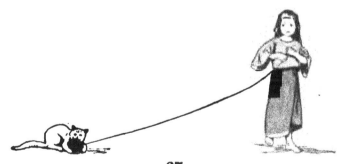

Is the boy playing?
No, he is working.
He is cutting grass.

Is Juan working?
Yes, Juan is working.
He is carrying grass.

Maria is working.
She is carrying fish.
What can you carry?

The carabao is working.
He is pulling the cart.

Aa Bb Cc Dd
Ee Fff Gg Hh
Ii Jj Kk Ll
Mm Nn Oo Pp
Qq Rrr Sss Tt
Uu Vv Ww Xx
Yy Zz

1 2 3 4 5 6 7 8 9 0

In writing, the pupils should form their letters and figures like those above. Writing lessons put on the board should follow the above models. Teach the alphabet from this page.

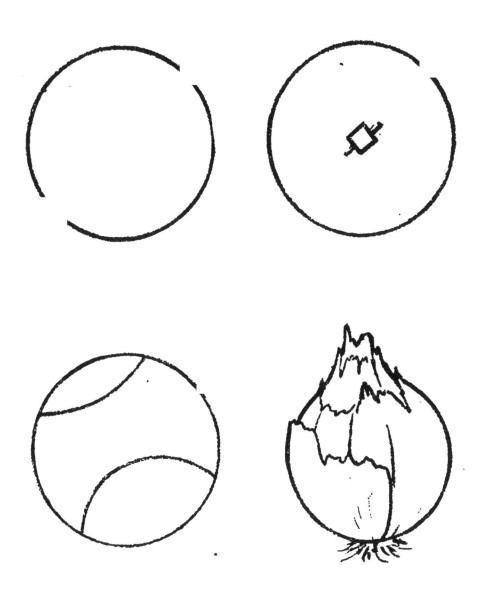

The following nine pages give a complete first year course in drawing based on the most common type forms. In drawings of this kind always draw the largest part first. In this case, draw the circle first.

Let the pupils find other objects shaped somewhat like a ball or sphere, and make drawings from them.

First sketch the outlines of these objects very lightly and add the inside lines last.

These drawing pages suggest only a few of the objects which may be used as models for drawing lessons.

Let the pupils find other objects shaped somewhat like a cube and make drawings directly from them.

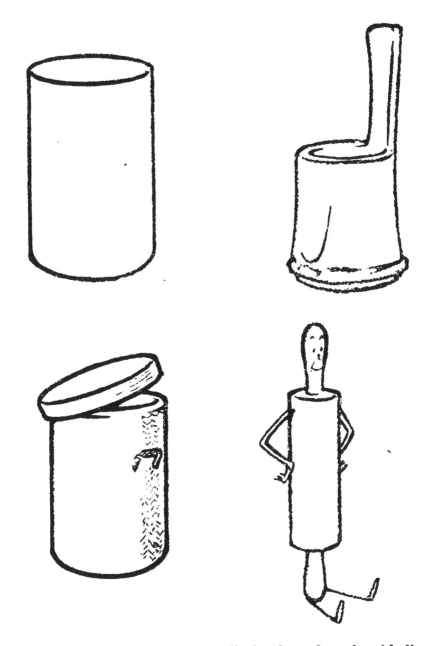

Draw the upper ellipse of a cylinder first, then the side lines, and last the bottom. Draw from other cylindrical objects.

44

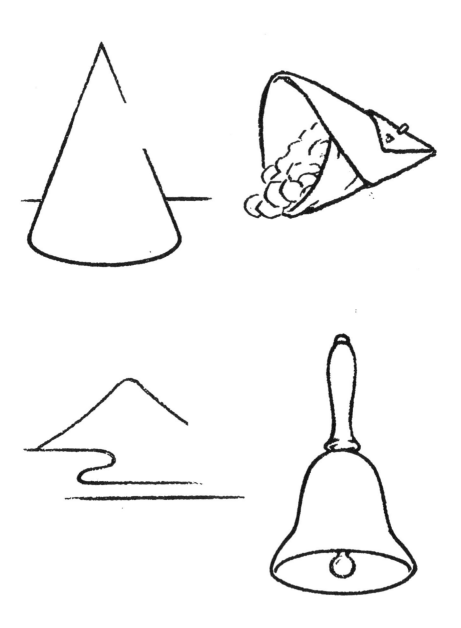

For a cone, draw a triangle first and then change the base
line into the half or the whole of an ellipse. Draw from other
conical objects.

This page gives a review of four type forms. When the figures have been drawn in outline, let the children fill in with small brush and ink.

Pupils may draw the above on slates or blackboard, using the broad side of pencil or chalk. Other animal figures may be cut or torn out of white paper.

Draw the head first, then the neck, body, legs, and arms. See what other actions of men and boys can be drawn in the same way.

knife	fork	spoon
plate	bottle	glass
cup saucer	pitcher bowl	dipper

table

chair

candle

flat-iron

pot
stove

broom

chest

key

lamp

50

house	roof	floor
wall	door	window
steps	post	gate fence

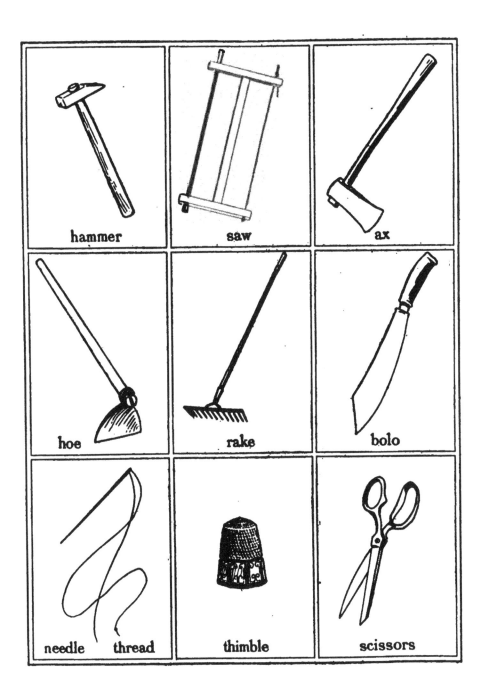

hammer

saw

ax

hoe

rake

bolo

needle   thread

thimble

scissors

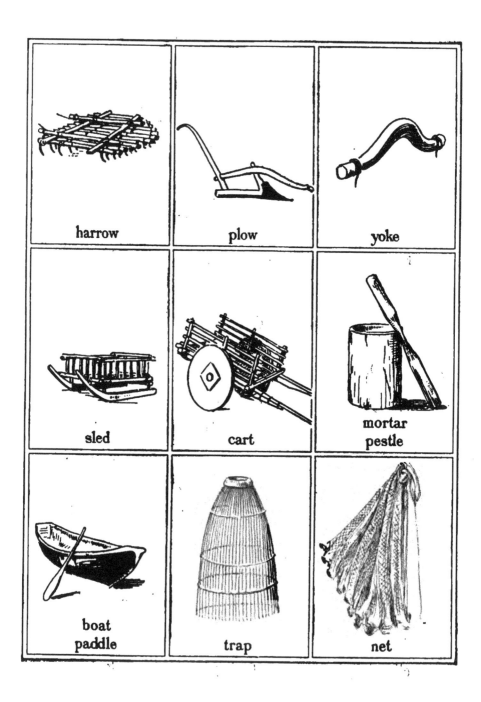

harrow	plow	yoke
sled	cart	mortar pestle
boat paddle	trap	net

running

crowing

climbing

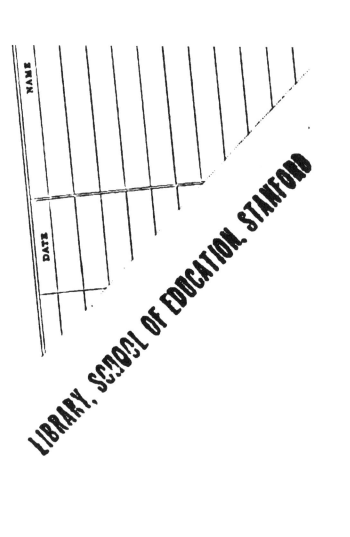

CPSIA information can be obtained
at www.ICGtesting.com
Printed in the USA
BVHW08*1526041018
529297BV00008B/159/P

9 780484 617215